JEREMY TAYLOR

LOVE ME BLINDLY

MICHAEL KNIERBEIN

Illustrations: Peter Bay Alexandersen

TEEN READERS · TR · TEEN READERS

Jeremy Taylor:
LOVE ME BLINDLY
Teen Readers, Level 3

Series editor: Ulla Malmmose

Editorial consultants:

Margaret Kersten, KLETT
Anna-Karin Vindal, GYLDENDAL NORSK FORLAG
Lars Madsen, SANTILLANA
Annemarie Zinck, ASCHEHOUG A/S
Ulla Malmmose, ASCHEHOUG A/S

ISBN Denmark 87-11-08604-1
www.easyreader.dk

Printed in Denmark by
Sangill Grafisk Produktion, Holme Olstrup

Biography of Jeremy Taylor

Jeremy Taylor was born in Bristol, England in 1962. He studied biology at London University and went on to teach biology in a school in London for a year. In January 1987 he left England for Mannheim, Germany. In March that year he bought an ex US army typewriter and, with the help of a girl he met in a pub, produced The English German Joke Book, his first book. The book was later published in Norway, Denmark, Spain and the Czech Republic.

In 1990, in need of a change, he left Germany for Egypt for two years, working as an English teacher at Mansoura University. While in Egypt he met some Czechs who said "You must visit our beautiful country." In August 1992 he did, and it was, so he has lived in the Czech Republic since then. He spends his time writing, juggling and travelling.

In addition to his joke books he has written a novel, 63 short stories, a juggling book, and a number of books for Egyptian children.

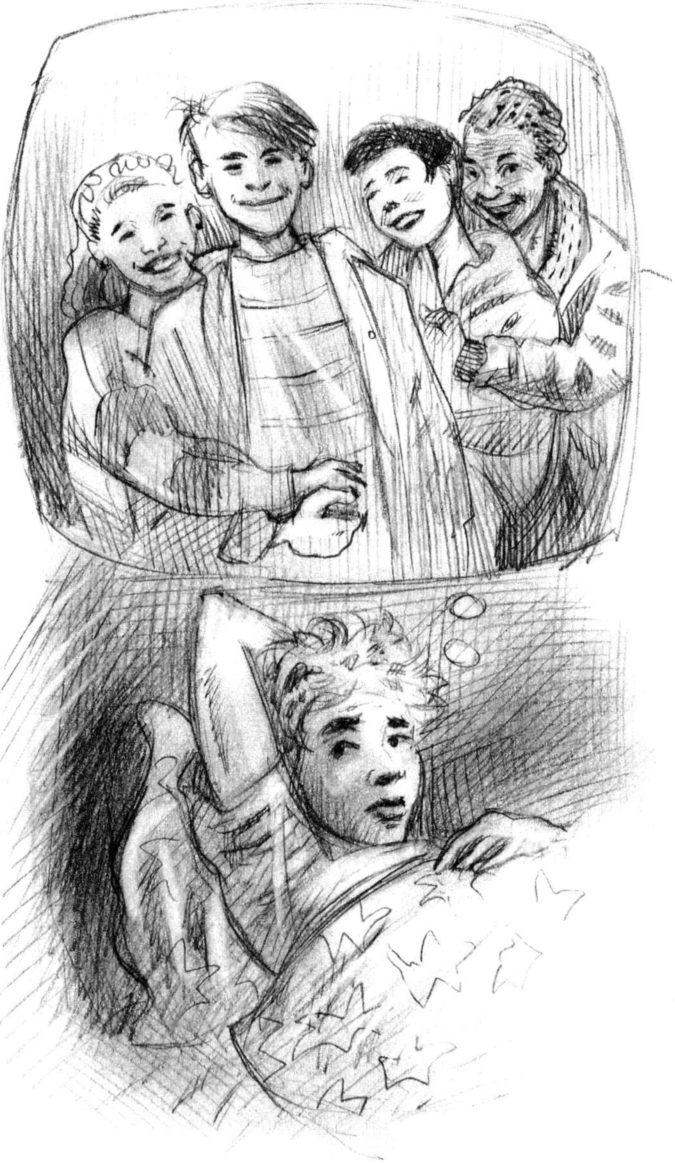

1

It was a Saturday morning and Tony Jackson was lying in bed, thinking about girlfriends. Alan Sutton had a girlfriend, Scott Terry had a girlfriend even Paul Bradshaw had a girlfriend. So why didn't he? This was a common subject of thought for Tony. In fact in his sixteen years on planet Earth he had only had one girlfriend. Sharon Luton had left him after a week. They hadn't even kissed! Life was *cruel*.

Today, thought Tony, will be a day of change. It was not New Year's day, or his birthday or any other day when people normally make *resolutions*. It was simply the tenth of September, but **this** tenth of September was to be a day of change. By the end of **this** tenth of September, Tony Daniel Jackson was going to have a girlfriend.

Over breakfast, Tony thought of a plan of action. He ate his corn flakes slowly and carefully. Then suddenly the idea hit him. He would go to the coffee bar in the centre of Waterbridge. He was sure to meet one of the girls from school. This was not a very new idea of Tony's. In fact he tried this same method almost every Saturday, but he felt that today was different. Today was going to be his lucky day.

---

cruel, hard, difficult
resolution, something important that someone has decided

2

When Tony got to Joe's bar, Scott Terry and Paul Bradshaw were already eating long *baguettes* full of cheese and salad. Tony sat down at their table.

"Hi, guys."

"Hi, TJ, what's new?"

"Today is a new day," said Tony dramatically. "Today is the first day of the rest of my life."

Scott and Paul looked at each other and both *shrugged* their shoulders. "Er, TJ, do you know something we don't?" asked Scott.

"Yes," said Tony. "Today I, Tony Daniel Jackson, am going to get myself a girlfriend."

Scott and Paul *groaned.* They had heard hundreds of such *declarations* from Tony. Still, it was fun to watch him try.

"So what method are you going to use this time?" asked Paul.

"You just wait and see," answered Tony. The reason that Tony answered 'you just wait and see' was because he was still thinking of a new plan, one that he hadn't tried more than two or three times before.

Suddenly Tony *grabbed* Scott's arm. "Look!"

"At what?"

"That girl over there!"

---

baguettes, long French bread
to shrug, to lift your shoulders
to groan, when you hear an old joke, you groan
declaration, something important that someone says
to grab, – to hold quickly

"Yes, Tony, it's a new girl in the fourth year. Don't tell me you're in love with her already."

"She's the most beautiful girl I have ever seen in my whole life."

Scott and Paul groaned again. Tony saw a new 'most beautiful girl in the world' on a fairly regular basis, usually about twice a week.

"So which plan are you going to use on this one, TJ?"

"You just wait and see," said Tony, his eyes following the girl as she made her way through the café, past the boys to the toilets.

On her way back, Tony's eyes were *fixed* on her.

---

fixed, here: not moving

"What are you staring at?"

"I am *gazing,*" said Tony dreamily, "at the most beautiful girl in the world."

"Dream on, dog *breath*! " The girl picked up a packet of sugar, dropped it into Tony's coffee and walked back to her table.

Scott and Paul almost wet themselves laughing.

"Dog breath!" laughed Scott, *slapping* his *thigh.*

"Woof! Woof!" barked Paul.

Tony watched them, trying his best not to look hurt. Well, maybe she wasn't **that** good looking anyway. Tony looked up and saw Sandra Long come into the cafe. She kissed Scott and sat on his *lap.*

"Hi, TJ, how are you these days?"

"Bad, Sandra, very bad."

"Still no girlfriend?"

"Not yet."

"Don't worry, there are plenty of fish in the sea."

"Yes, but I haven't got a very good *fishing rod,*" answered Tony.

fishing rod

"One day a fish will just jump out of the water into your arms."

---

to gaze, to look at for a long time
breath, the air that comes out of your mouth
to slap, to hit with a flat hand
thigh, the muscles in the top part of your legs
lap, when your thighs are horizontal they form your lap

"Yes," said Tony, "and pigs will fly."

"Toasted cheese sandwich?"

"Here," said Tony.

The waitress leant over and put the toasted cheese sandwich in front of Tony.

"Thanks," said Tony, rather weakly.

"Don't tell me . . ." said Scott.

"That girl," said Tony, "smiled at me. She had the most beautiful smile in the world."

"Tony, not two in one day, please," said Paul.

"I've got a plan," said Tony, watching the waitress's every move around the cafe.

When it was time to pay, Tony collected the money together and then *scribbled* a little note on the bill.

The waitress took it away and brought back the change and a piece of paper. Tony picked it up quickly and read the three lines.

1. I hate James Bond films.
2. My boyfriend is taking me out tonight.
3. You're not my type anyway.

---

to scribble, to write quickly

3

'There must be a way,' thought Tony to himself as he walked along Waterbridge High Street. After what had happened in the café he felt terrible.

"Excuse me, is the library around here somewhere?"

"Yes, it's over there, can't you see it?"

"No, I'm blind," said the young man next to Tony.

"Oh I'm very sorry, I didn't mean to ..."

"It's all right. People forget that young people can be blind as well. I'm probably only a year or two older than you."

"*Er*, do you want some help getting across the road?"

"If you wouldn't mind, I hate this High Street."

"I'm not surprised. I sometimes have difficulty crossing it and I'm not blind."

Tony held the older boy's arm and walked him to the edge of the *pavement*.

"Er, if you don't mind, can I take **your** arm?"

"Oh, sorry."

"When someone takes my arm I feel I am being *arrested* by the police."

Tony and the blind boy walked between two cars and then made it across the road.

"Thanks a lot, by the way, my name's Eddie," said Eddie.

---

er, when you can't think of what to say, you can say 'er'
pavement, the side of a street where you can walk
to arrest, when the police find someone they think is a criminal, they sometimes arrest him (or her)

"And I'm Tony, but my friends call me TJ."

"Okay, TJ, I'll see you around."

"Um, Eddie, you might think this is a *dumb* question, but why are you going into the library?"

"I'm doing some research for a novel I'm writing."

"You're writing a novel?"

---

dumb, here: stupid

"Yeah, normally I write non-fiction, but I want to be more creative."

"Yes, but how . . ."

"How do I read the books in the library?"

"Yeah."

"Well Waterbridge has the biggest collection of books in *Braille* in the area, that's why I'm here. I live in Greenbrook."

"Okay, I'll let you get on with your work, hope to see you again sometime," said Tony.

"Thanks for the help!" called Eddie before disappearing into Waterbridge library.

Braille, system of printing for the blind, using raised dots

4

Later that evening, Tony was walking along Waterbridge High Street with a bag of fish and chips when he saw Eddie again. He was about to call out to him when a young woman went up to Eddie. They spoke

and then the girl took Eddie's arm. Eddie dropped his hand and took the girl's arm. They crossed over the High Street still talking to each other. Tony could not hear what they were saying but suddenly the girl laughed. Tony continued on the other side of the street, watching Eddie and his new friend. Outside Joe's bar they stopped. They talked for a little while longer and then disappeared inside.

Tony stopped walking. He could feel *butterflies* playing football inside him. He felt like a *volcano* about to *erupt.* His brain worked faster than it ever did at school. He had an idea. It was an *acorn* inside his head and it was growing. Tony walked slowly in the direction of home. Within minutes his acorn had grown into a *sapling* and by the time he got to his house he had a tall oak tree trying to break out of his head.

the volcano is erupting

acorn

butterfly, a small insect with beautiful wings. To have butterflies in your stomach means to be nervous. The 'butterflies' are adrenalin
sapling, a small tree

5

"Can I help you, young man?"

"Oh, er, yes, thank you. I'm trying to cross the road."

The old man took the blind boy's arm.

"Excuse me, do you mind if **I** take **your** arm. I feel like I'm being arrested if someone takes my arm."

"I'm sorry," said the old man. "I didn't realise. Where exactly are you trying to get to?"

"To Ballston library, I'm, er, researching a novel."

"Oh well, it's not far to go, another fifty yards on the left."

"Thank you very much."

"What's your name? If you write a bestseller I can tell my *mates* in the pub that I met you."

"Tony," said Tony. "But my friends call me TJ."

"Well good luck, TJ."

cane

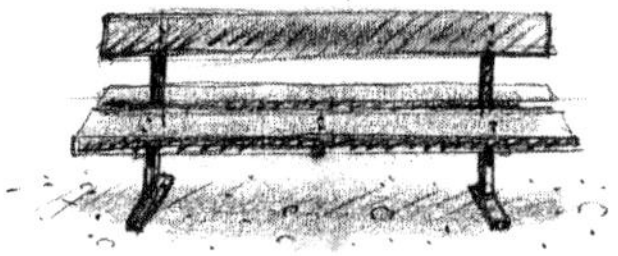

bench

---

mate, a friend

6

Tony waited until the old man was out of sight. He kept tapping his white *cane* in front of him. He felt very stupid. People stared at him as he walked very slowly along the pavement. Did people always stare at blind people? He sat down on the *bench* outside the library. He had a football magazine in his pocket which he would have loved to have started reading. However he pulled out a banana and started eating it.

"Car accident, was it?" An old lady had sat down next to him.

"Um, yes," said Tony.

"I'm not surprised, the way young people drive these days," said the old lady. " My sister's nearly blind. But she's over seventy. I read the newspaper to her sometimes."

"That's very kind of you."

"Been blind long, have you?"

"Um, about three months now," replied a nervous Tony.

"You're very nervous," said the old lady.

"It's ... it's my first time..out on my own. It's not easy getting around with a white stick instead of two eyes."

"Mmm, I suppose not."

The old lady took out a large handkerchief and blew into it. She then *inspected* the results of her actions. Tony watched her out of the side of his dark glasses.

---

to inspect, to look at carefully

Why couldn't he be as lucky as Eddie? One nice old man and one not so nice old woman, where were all the beautiful young girls of Ballston?

"Hello, TJ." It was the old man who had helped him earlier. "Having a rest, are you?"

"Yes, I've got a lot of work I'd like to do today."

"He's only been blind three months, traffic accident," the old lady informed the old man.

"You're very *brave* to be on your own just three months after your accident," said the old man.

"Today's his first day. He is nervous, aren't you, dear?" The old lady touched Tony's arm.

"Yes, a little."

"I've got to be going," the old lady informed Tony and the old man. "The over sixties club starts in half an hour."

"Have a nice time," called Tony.

"Do you *want a hand* getting into the library? I'm going in myself now."

"Er, well ..."

"Come on, I'll give you a hand."

The old man held his arm next to Tony's and Tony put his hand around the old man's arm.

"Careful now, there are five steps."

Tony felt his way forward with his white stick and then with his shoes. Sometimes he closed his eyes but quickly opened them again. Being blind was not easy.

---

brave, having courage, not frightened
to want a hand, to want some help

7

In fact, being blind was very, very difficult. At the library, the old man would not leave him alone. They had gone up to the desk together and Tony asked if they had any books in Braille. His heart was beating faster than ever when the librarian went to look.

It was not easy for him to hide his happiness when she returned to apologise for not having any books in Braille, saying that he would have to go to Waterbridge library.

Tony thanked both the librarian and the old man and left as quickly as a blind boy could. Outside the library there were some boys playing football. As Tony was walking along, the ball rolled in his direction.

"Hey, mister, can ... oh sorry."

Tony stopped the ball with his foot and then *chipped* it into the boy's arms.

"Wow! Guys, did you see that?"

Tony could see the other boys watching him as he continued *shuffling* along the road. He had to get out of sight of everyone so that he could become *sighted* again.

It was in the lane on the way to the railway station that Tony was finally sure that he was not being watched. Carefully he looked behind him and then took off his dark glasses and put his white stick under a bush.

---

to chip, to kick the ball into the air but not very far
to shuffle, here: to walk slowly
sighted, able to see

On the train on the way home he thought about what he was doing. On the one hand it was nothing more than a *harmless* bit of acting. On the other hand it was dangerous game which could get him into serious trouble. He would try another town tomorrow after school.

---

harmless, not dangerous

8

In the next three days, Tony tried three towns around Waterbridge. He was terrified of being recognised. He wore an old coat that he hadn't worn for ages and a baseball cap to cover his curly, blond hair. His dark glasses were a pair of his mum's old sunglasses.

In three evenings he had been helped by *numerous* old people and quite a few middle-aged people. Why did young people avoid people who were blind? The biggest *scare* so far happened in New Wellington. He had been walking along through the shopping centre when a woman came up to him. "Tony? Tony Jackson?"

"Yes? Who is it?" Tony could see it was a middle-aged woman with short dark hair. He nearly took off his glasses so that he could see her better.

"I'm Mrs Spencer, David's mum, we used to live in Waterbridge."

"Hello, Mrs Spencer, how is David these days?"

"Oh he's fine," said Mrs Spencer, feeling *guilty* about her answer. "I didn't know about your . . ."

"My eyes?"

"Yes, what happened?"

"Car accident."

"Oh that's terrible. David will be very sad to hear that."

"Actually, Mrs Spencer, I'd rather you didn't tell

---

numerous, very many
to scare, to frighten
guilty, here: bad

anyone. I'd rather people remembered me as I was."

"Tony, you're talking as though you were dead."

'I will be if people find out what I'm doing,' thought Tony.

9

It was on the fifth day that Tony's luck changed. He had already given up and was on his way back to the train station. It was getting cold and dark. Wearing sun glasses in the dark meant that there was added realism to Tony's slow walk. He was about to take off his glasses and hide his stick when he heard footsteps behind him. He wanted to look behind to see who it was but had to keep acting blind.

"Lovely evening," said the girl.

"Yes, maybe the last warm evening of the year," replied Tony.

"Are you going to the station?"

"Er, yes," said Tony, who wanted to become sighted again.

"Where are you going?"

"To Waterbridge."

"What a coincidence, so am I," said the girl. "My aunt lives there."

Tony's interest in the girl suddenly stopped. She was going to Waterbridge. They would travel on the same train. He wouldn't be able to get rid of his dark glasses and white stick before they got to his home town. What if someone recognised him?

"Have you got a ticket already?"

"Yes, I've got a return ticket."

"I'll have to buy one." The girl disappeared off to the ticket office. Tony looked around. What could he do? Where could he go?

"Hi, I'm back!"

He was too late.

"Is the train here yet?"

"Not yet, but it'll be arriving on platform two. We'll have to go through the *subway*. Would you like some help?"

This was the first time the girl had *treated* him any differently from a sighted person.

subway, a passage under a road (or a railway track)
to treat, here: behave towards, regard

"Er, yes please, do you think I could hold your arm?"

"Sure." The girl held her arm next to Tony's and he put his hand around her arm. Still feeling the ground in front of him with his white stick, Tony and the girl made their way to the subway steps.

"My name's Julia," said Julia as the train pulled away.

"My name's Tony, but my friends call me TJ," said Tony.

"So can I call you 'TJ'?"

"Sure, if I can call you Julia."

The light in the train was just enough for Tony to be able *to make out* Julia's face. She had *wavy* black hair and smooth brown skin. She had high *cheekbones* and lovely white teeth. She had an accent, which, she told him, was because her mother was Greek and she had spent the first eleven years of her life in Greece.

"We're just coming in to Waterbridge," announced Julia.

"Already?" asked Tony, who was enjoying talking to Julia and was not looking forward to arriving in Waterbridge.

"Listen, TJ," said Julia as they walked through Waterbridge station. "I'm sure you're very busy writing your novel and I don't know if you'd want to see me ... I mean **be** with me again, but what are you doing on Sunday?"

---

to make out, here: to see (with difficulty)
wavy, not straight but not curly
cheekbones, the bones in your face under your eyes

"Not a lot, why?" said Tony, trying to keep out of the lights.

"Well I know a little lake near New Wellington. I wondered if you'd like to come swimming with me?"

"Well, I'm not sure that ..." Tony saw a hopeful smile on Julia's face. It reminded him of the girl in Joe's café, only Julia's smile was more beautiful. "What time on Sunday?"

"Shall we say 10 o'clock, at New Wellington station?"

"I'll be there."

10

"What is wrong with TJ?" Scott, Sandra and Paul sat in the school canteen and watched Tony as he waited in the *queue* for his dinner.

"He looks a bit like Fred Astaire in that film, Singing in the Rain," said Paul.

"Except he hasn't got an umbrella," said Sandra.

"And it's not raining," added Scott. "And anyway, it wasn't Fred Astaire, it was Gene Kelly."

"All right, all right, he looks happy and he's dancing, but why?"asked Paul.

"I have an idea," said Sandra. "I think he's in love again. Girl number seventy five this week."

"Ah but this one is special," said Paul, *imitating* Tony. "She's the most wonderful girl he's ever seen in his whole life."

Tony picked up his *tray* of food and brought it over to his friends' table, still moving as though he were wearing a Walkman.

"Everything all right, is it, TJ?" asked Scott.

"Never been better," said Tony, starting on his goulash and potatoes.

"A new girl in your life *by any chance*?" asked Paul.

"Yes, the most beautiful girl in the world."

Sandra, Scott and Paul all groaned.

"And what does she think of you?" asked Sandra.

---

queue, a line of people
to imitate, to act in the same way as someone
tray, thin board of metal or plastic, used to carry things
by any chance, here: perhaps

“She likes me.”

“She must be blind!” said Scott, which made Sandra and Paul laugh.

‘If only you knew,’ thought Tony.

“So when can we meet . . . ?”

“Julia? You can’t.”

“Why not?” asked Sandra

“Because she doesn’t exist, that’s why not,” said Paul. “She’s just an idea in TJ’s wild imagination.”

“She doesn’t live in Waterbridge,” answered Tony, staring at Paul.

“But why don’t you invite her to Joe’s on Saturday?” suggested Sandra. “I’d like to meet her.”

“Maybe one day,” said Tony.

11

"Hi, TJ, it's good to see you again."

"Hi, Julia. It's good to s . . . be with you again."

As TJ and Julia walked away from the train, the ticket inspector *scratched* his head. He was sure he had seen that boy running for the train at Waterbridge.

"So how far is it?"

"To the lake? Not far. It'll take us about ten minutes."

It was a warm day. Julia was wearing a tee shirt. Tony held her arm and enjoyed the touch of her soft skin. Julia talked of her school and her hobbies. She collected old postcards and her favourite subject at school was biology.

"We might see some *newts* in the lake."

Oops! Julia felt bad every time she mentioned seeing things. It must be so difficult for Tony. He was so brave.

"Are we there yet?" asked Tony when he saw the lake ahead of him.

"Yes we are, you're very good at judging time," complimented Julia. She led Tony along a path at the side of the lake. They came to a sunny *clearing*.

"Well, here we are!"said Julia. "The lake is about five metres in front of you. Are you ready for a swim?"

"Yes, yes, I haven't had a swim since . . ."

---

to scratch, if your dog has fleas, it will scratch itself
newt, a small animal that lives in water. It looks like a cross between a fish and a frog
clearing, small part of a forest with no trees

Julia touched his arm. She smiled a smile which she thought Tony couldn't see.

"Time for a swim!" said Julia. She put down her bag and pulled off her tee shirt.

"Come on, TJ, don't just stand there!"

Tony watched Julia adjusting her bathing suit. Then he put down his white stick and took off his trousers. Underneath he was wearing his colourful swimming trunks. He then took off his jacket and lifted off his tee shirt.

"Hey, you've got a good body," said Julia, as she removed her shoes and socks.

'And so have you,' thought Tony to himself.

"Aren't you going to take your glasses off?"

"Er, I'd rather not. You see my eyes are not a pretty sight."

"I understand," said Julia.

Julia and Tony swam for about twenty minutes. They swam to the small island in the middle of the lake. Although it was September, the water was still quite warm. Julia was an excellent swimmer and on their way back she showed Tony her lifesaving skills.

After swimming they lay in the sun. It was surprisingly warm. Tony hoped that Julia would ask him to rub sun cream into her back.

"TJ, will you rub some sun cream into my back? I don't want to burn today."

'This,' thought Tony, 'is Paradise.'

"You're very good at massage, TJ," said Julia. "Perhaps you could become a full time masseur. I've heard quite a few blind people study massage and physiotherapy. Blind people have such *sensitive* fingers. Mmm, that feels good!"

---

sensitive, full of feeling

12

"Hi, TJ, I'm glad you could make it."

"No problem. My parents encourage me to go out. But I'm still not *convinced* about your idea."

"Don't worry. There's only one film on in New Wellington this week and you've probably seen it before."

"What is it?"

"The Sound of Music. I thought it would be good for you as you probably know most of the songs."

Tony knew the film very well. He had seen it three or four times before. He always cried at the end, the part where the nuns take out parts from the Nazis' car.

"We should hurry or we'll be late."

When they arrived, the advertisements were being shown.

"Oh it's very dark," said Julia, "but that's no problem for you, TJ . . . TJ? Where are you?"

Tony was still wearing his dark glasses when they entered the darkened cinema. He was getting better at using his white stick but not well enough. He had *tripped* and fallen down the steps between the rows of seats. His glasses came off and his white stick *snapped*.

"Are you all right, TJ?", asked Julia as she helped him up off the floor.

"Yes, I'm fine, just embarrassed," said Tony.

Both Tony and Julia enjoyed the film. Tony still cried

---

to be convinced, to be sure
to trip, to fall over something
to snap, to break

when the nuns went to the Mother Superior, "Forgive me for I have sinned . . ."

A little tear rolled out of Tony's eye. Julia leant over and brushed it away. She squeezed Tony's hand and he squeezed Julia's in return. They were still holding hands when they left the cinema.

13

"Look at TJ!"

Scott, Sandra and Paul sat in the canteen. They watched as Tony stood in the queue. He had a large smile on his face and he looked around dreamily.

"He looks like he's in love," said Scott.

"I'm in love," said Tony as he joined his friends.

"With one of the canteen ladies?" suggested Paul. "They're a bit old for you, TJ."

"Are you still together with Julia?" asked Sandra.

"Yes, and I will be forever," said Tony.

"Don't forget, forever is about a week, TJ," said Paul.

"Not for me and Julia," said Tony. "We're in love."

"How do you know she loves you?"

"She told me."

"When?"

"While we were walking to New Wellington station."

"And she said, 'TJ, I love you,'?"

"That's right," answered Tony.

"TJ, am I right in thinking Julia lives in New Wellington?" asked Scott.

"You are."

"Then why did **she** walk with **you** to the station instead of **you** walking **her** home?"

Tony's brain worked quickly. "She . . . left her bike at the station. She had to pick it up."

"So when are you going to see her again?" asked Sandra.

"On Saturday, we're going *tandem* riding."

---

tandem, a bicycle for two people

"Tandem riding? But you haven't got a tandem."

"No, but Julia's brother has got one," answered Tony.

Scott, Paul and Sandra looked at each other and shook their heads. It was *amazing*. Tony Jackson had found a girlfriend.

---

amazing, here: surprising

14

"Ready?"

"I'm ready," replied Tony.

The tandem *wobbled* as Tony and Julia set off down the road. Gary, Julia's brother, watched nervously as they went around their first bend. Tony, sitting right behind Julia, was terrified. He wanted to *steer* like a normal bike but on a tandem, only the person in front can steer. The person at the back simply has to pedal.

After a few curves, Tony began to enjoy himself. It was an amazing feeling rushing through the country-side around New Wellington sitting right behind Julia. He even closed his eyes for a few hundred metres but opened them again when they came to a curve.

They had a quick picnic in some woodland. Some dark clouds were moving above them. It was much cooler than the previous weekend. On their way home it started to rain. At first it was not too bad and they kept going but then the rain came down harder and harder and Julia put on the *brakes* and stopped the tandem at the side of the road.

"I can't see a thing!" said Julia.

"Nor can I!" said Tony.

"Oh TJ," said Julia throwing her arms around Tony, "I love you so much."

---

to wobble, to move from side to side
to steer, to control the direction of a bicycle (or car)
brakes, you use your brakes when you want to stop your bicycle (or car)

15

They spent the rest of the afternoon in a *bus shelter* playing 'Who am I?' First of all Julia thought of a famous person and Tony had to guess who she was thinking of. He could ask questions but she was only allowed to answer yes or no. After 16 questions, Tony guessed correctly, Tom Cruise. It took just 9 questions for Julia to work out that Tony was thinking of Julius Caesar. After seven questions, Tony was still having problems with Julia's second person.

"So she's American, you're not sure if she's alive or dead but you think she's dead. She's not an actress, she isn't a sportswoman, she's not an artist, she's written some books but she's not famous as a writer."

"That's right."

Tony had no idea who it was. He could not think of any other things she could be. "I give up."

"You give up? Already?"

"I'm sorry. I can't think who it is."

"Helen Keller*!"

"Helen who?"

"Helen Keller. The famous deaf, *dumb* and blind girl. She learnt to read and write in Braille despite the fact that she couldn't hear, speak or see."

"Wow, a *talented* girl."

---

bus shelter, a little building where you can wait for a bus
* See text, page 61
dumb, here: not able to speak.
talented, to be able to do something very well

"Talking of talented girls, I've got a present for you."

Julia reached into her bag and took out an envelope. She held Tony's hand and put the envelope into it.

"Shall I open it now?"

"Sure, we've got at least an hour before this rain stops."

Tony opened the envelope and took out the piece of paper inside. The paper was blank but it was covered with hundreds of little bumps. Luckily, Tony recognised it. "It's Braille!"

"Go on read it!" said Julia excitedly.

Tony's brain worked fast. What could he do? He

put the paper on his knees and ran his fingers over the little bumps line by line. He smiled. "Thank you, Julia," he said when he reached what he thought was the end. "That's a lovely message."

"And what's the answer?"

"The answer?"

"The answer to my question?"

"You'll have to wait for the answer."

Tony put the message inside his jacket pocket. "How did you do it? I mean, how did you write the note?"

"An old lady in the village is blind. She has got a special Braille typewriter. I typed it out on that."

"Julia, you're amazing," said Tony.

"I know," said Julia.

16

As soon as he got home, Tony *rushed off* to the library. He had one hour before it closed. He took out a book on blindness and quickly turned the pages. On page 173 he found what he was looking for. There was the Braille alphabet. He took out Julia's note and started writing down the letters.

D-E-A-R T-J, I H-O-P-E Y-O-U L-I-K-E M-E A-S M-U-C-H A-S I L-I-K-E Y-O-U. W-O-U-L-D Y-O-U L-I-K-E T-O H-A-V-E D-I-N-N-E-R W-I-T-H M-E T-O-N-I-G-H-T? M-E-E-T M-E A-T T-H-E I-T-A-L-I-A-N P-I-Z-Z-A R-E-S-T-A-U-R-A-N-T I-N N-W A-T S-E-V-E-N O'-C-L-O-C-K. L-O-V-E J-U-L-I-A.

At seven o'clock? thought Tony. It was already five to six. He jumped on his bike and pedalled home quickly. He had a shower, brushed his teeth and combed his hair. Then he jumped back on his bike and pedalled off to the station.

As usual he left his bike in a bush near the station, then he took out his white stick and dark glasses and went into the station.

"Excuse me, when is the next train to New Wellington?"

"It's just gone," said the woman on the platform. "The next one is at ten past seven."

"Oh no!" Tony's brain worked quickly. There was only one thing for it.

---

to rush off, to go quickly

The woman on the platform watched open-mouthed as the blind boy ran up the steps into the station. A minute later she saw him cycling as fast as he could towards New Wellington. The woman shook her head and sat down. She had been working too hard lately.

17

Tony arrived in New Wellington at three minutes to seven. He jumped off his bike and hid it under some bushes. Then he took out his stick and his dark glasses and made his way as quickly as possible to the pizza restaurant.

When he arrived he wasn't sure what to do. He had never been into a restaurant 'blind' before. As he walked past the window he looked in trying to see Julia. It was quite dark in the restaurant but he was sure she would be inside.

She wasn't. Tony stood in the doorway waiting for Julia to come and help him. He couldn't go running around the restaurant looking for her.

"Can I help you?"

"Er, yes, I'm meeting my girlfriend here. Her name is Julia . . ." Tony felt stupid as he didn't know Julia's surname.

"Would you like to sit and wait for her?"

"Yes please."

Tony sat down and accepted the offer of a glass of mineral water from the waiter. When Julia came in at half past seven, Tony very nearly jumped up and *hugged* her.

"TJ, you're here already!"

"Hi Julia, your note said seven o'clock."

"I know, I've been waiting at the station for you since quarter to seven. How did you get here? "

---

to hug, to put your arms around someone

Tony's brain worked quickly. "Er, my dad brought me."

"Your dad? It's strange, you very rarely talk about your family or your friends. I'd really like to meet them. It's a pity about your telephone. When did you say the phone company are going to repair it?"

"We're not sure, it could be days, it could be weeks, it could even be months."

Eating blind was a whole new experience for Tony. He had to feel for his glass every time he took a drink. When he wanted salt or pepper he had to ask Julia. Just one mistake and she would know everything. Still his quattro stagioni pizza was good and Julia enjoyed her pizza formaggio.

"I've got a good idea," announced Julia after the meal. "What are you doing on Saturday afternoon?"

"I hope I'm going to see you," said Tony. "Well, **be** with you."

"Have you ever been bowling?"

"Bowling?"

"Yes, bowling, you know, ten pins and a big ball, you throw the ball and try to knock down the pins. The bowling club has special *rates* on Saturday afternoons. I thought it might be fun."

"Okay, I'll give it a try. What time shall we meet?"

"Two o'clock, at the station?"

"I'll be there," said Tony.

---

rates, here: prices

18

"So, TJ, how is it going with Julia?"

"Very well thank you, Scott. We're going bowling on Saturday."

"Bowling?"

"Yes, bowling, you know, ten pins and a big ball, you throw the ball and try to knock down the pins."

"Yes, yes, I know what bowling is, I'm just surprised. Are you going to the one in New Wellington?"

"Yes," said Tony, a little nervously. "Why do you ask? "

"Well, it's Sandra's birthday on Saturday and I'm taking her there with Paul and Cathy. It should be a lot of fun."

"Saturday afternoon?"

"Yes, about two o'clock."

"Julia?"

19

"TJ! What a surprise! I thought your phone was broken."

"It is, I'm calling from a friend's house," lied Tony.

"Listen Julia, about Saturday."

"I'm looking forward to it."

"Well, I'm afraid we'll have to *postpone* it."

"But why? "

Tony's brain worked hard. "It's my mum. She's just come out of hospital. I want to be with her."

"You didn't tell me she was in hospital," said Julia.

"Well, I don't want you to worry about my problems," lied Tony. "Do you think we could postpone it until Sunday afternoon?"

"Well, okay, but I had a surprise for you. I have a friend that I think you would like to meet."

"A friend? Who is it?"

"It's a surprise. You'll have to wait until Sunday."

---

to postpone, to cancel or stop something until a later date

20

Tony woke up on Sunday morning a little nervous. Normally he loved being with Julia but today was somehow different. Who was her friend? It wasn't any of his friends from school. He had met them on Saturday night. They had been quite disappointed that they had not met Julia at the bowling centre. TJ explained that Julia's mother had just come out of hospital and that Julia wanted to be with her.

"TJ! Hi!"

"Hi, Julia," said Tony as he got off the train. They kissed and went through the station and along New Wellington High Street together.

"My friend is going to meet us at the bowling centre," said Julia, squeezing Tony's hand.

"Great," lied Tony. "I can't wait."

Julia led Tony past the park. Some girls were playing baseball. Tony watched them out of the side of his dark glasses. They were pretty good. Finally they got to the bowling centre. They found their *bowling alley* and took off their coats ready to start bowling.

"I'm not sure where my friend is," said Julia. "But I'm sure he'll be along soon."

bowling alley

'He', thought Tony. 'Has she got another boy-friend?' Tony's head was full of ideas as Julia led him up to the alley for his first *attempt* at bowling. She put the large ball in his hand and showed him how to hold the ball with the holes. She got him to swing the ball

attempt, try

and then stood back as Tony let go of the ball. People bowling nearby stopped and watched as Tony's ball at first bounced and then rolled down the alley. Seven of the pins fell down. People around him *applauded.*

"Er, how did I do?"

"Seven down, that's amazing for someone who **can** see."

Tony thought he was doing a bit too well so the next two balls went off to the side without hitting any more pins.

"Ah here's my friend now," said Julia.

Tony's heart began to beat faster. He turned round slowly and then jumped backwards.

"So TJ, I'd like you to meet Eddie. Eddie, this is TJ."

Julia brought the two hands together and Eddie and TJ shook hands.

"You guys sit down for a while, I'll get some drinks," said Julia and she disappeared off to the bar.

"So, we meet again."

"So you remember me?"

"Of course I do."

"You must think I'm bad doing what I'm doing, but please, don't tell Julia. I love her and I'm fairly sure she loves me. If she found out I'm not blind . . . well, I don't know what she would say."

"Did you want sugar in your coffee, TJ?"

Tony jumped. "Er, no thanks."

"Do you think you can go your whole life *pretending* you're blind?"

---

to applaud, to clap your hands
to pretend, to act like someone, to imitate

"Well no, but Julia is my first real girlfriend and I'm worried about losing her. She means a lot to me."

"From what she tells me, you mean a lot to her, too."

"So what should I do?"

"You'll have to tell her."

"Are you crazy? She'll leave me!"

"If she loves you when you're blind, why shouldn't she love you when you can see?"

"Because I lied to her, I tricked her."

"Do you want to go on lying to her and tricking her for ever?"

"No, but . . ."

"So, one coffee, with no sugar, one mineral water and one tomato juice."

"Thanks, Julia."

"Right, now let's get on with some serious bowling."

21

Tony and Julia left the bowling centre at four o'clock. Tony took Julia's arm and they walked slowly along the street together.

"Julia?"

"Yes, TJ?"

"There's something I want to tell you."

"Yes, TJ?"

"I'm not sure how to put it into words."

"Take your time."

"It's just that ..."

"Is it about your mum?"

"No, no, it's about us, you and me."

"Yes, TJ?"

Out of the corner of his eye, TJ could see the girls still playing baseball.

"I want to tell you that ..."

Suddenly a baseball flew towards them.

"Look out!" shouted one of the girls.

Tony could see where the ball was going. It was about to hit Julia on the side of the face. Tony's brain worked faster than it ever had before. His right hand shot up and caught the ball, centimetres from Julia's left eye.

Julia stopped.

"You know, don't you?" said Tony.

Julia nodded, then she began to laugh.

"What's so funny?"

"You, TJ?"

"Aren't you mad at me?"

Julia was laughing so much she could only shake her head.

"You mean, you're not going to leave me?"

Julia shook her head again. Tony and Julia sat down on a bench in the park, every time Julia looked at Tony she started laughing.

"How long have you known?"

"A long time," said Julia, slowly bringing herself under control. "Do you remember that time when you fell down the steps in the cinema?"

"Yes," said Tony.

"Your glasses came off but you reached straight out and picked them up again."

"I . . . I'm sorry."

"That evening, you were at the station and I was about to go home, then I remembered that I had some chocolates for you. When I went back into the station, there you were, looking at the timetable!"

"Oh no!" said Tony.

"And do you remember the note I gave you in Braille?"

"Yes."

"Do you remember you said I was amazing?"

"Yes."

"Well I wanted to tell you that **you** were amazing. You were trying to read it upside down!"

Even Tony had to laugh then.

"But why didn't you say something? Why did you let me make a fool of myself?"

"It was fun. I enjoyed it."

"But I tricked you, I lied to you. I don't deserve you," said Tony, hoping that what Eddie had said was true.

"I don't mind if you can see or if you can't see," said Julia, putting her arms around Tony. "I still love you blindly."

Questions

Chapters 1 to 7

1. In chapter two, Sandra tells TJ that a "fish will just jump out of the water into your arms". TJ replies, "Yes, and pigs will fly." What are they talking about?
2. The waitress wrote three lines to TJ. What do you think TJ wrote to the waitress?
3. What does TJ see that gives him his good idea?
4. When you started reading chapter five, did you think it was Eddie or TJ, trying to cross the road?
5. Describe the old man. Describe the old lady.

Chapters 8 to 21

1. Who is David Spencer?
2. Have you seen The Sound of Music? Did you cry at the end?
3. At the end of chapter 16, why does the woman in the station think she has been working too hard?
4. TJ had not heard of Helen Keller, have you? Have you read the book called 'The Miracle Worker' about her amazing life?
5. Why is TJ's telephone 'broken'?
6. Why does TJ call Julia to postpone their bowling?
7. What do you think of Eddie?
8. Do you know a boy, or a girl who might do something like TJ did?

What do you think?

1. What do you think TJ's friends thought of him?
2. Do you think TJ's method of getting a girlfriend was a good one?
3. If you had been a friend of TJ's and had found out what he was doing, would you have told him to stop?
4. Do you think Julia should have left TJ when she found out he was tricking her?
5. Why do you think she didn't?
6. Do you think there are pressures on young people to have a boyfriend or girlfriend? Where does the pressure come from? Is it from parents? From friends? From television and magazines?
7. Do you think it is easier or harder for blind people to find boyfriends and girlfriends?
8. How different would it be having a boyfriend or girlfriend that was blind? What would you do with him/her?
9. If you are a girl, would you like TJ as your boyfriend? If you are a boy, would you like Julia as your girlfriend? In both cases, explain your answer.
10. Has the story changed the way you think of blind people?

The Life of Helen Keller

Helen Adams Keller was born in Alabama in America in 1880. She was a normal baby but when she was 19 months old she became very ill. After her illness she could not see and could not hear. Many people thought that she was stupid. She cried a lot because no one understood her.

Then one day a woman called Anne Sullivan came to see Helen. Anne Sullivan was a very special teacher. She took Helen's hand and held it under some water. Then she touched Helen's fingers in a special way. This was 'water' in a language for people who cannot hear or see. Helen understood this and wanted to know more words. Each day she learned more and more things. Helen Keller was not stupid. She was a very intelligent woman. She graduated (with honours) from Radcliffe College in 1904.

She spent her life writing books and travelling the world, trying to help other deaf and blind people. She died in 1968 at the age of 88.

Would you like to read more about her amazing life? Her books have been translated into many languages. Ask in your library for books by or about a very special woman called Helen Keller.